Fashion Design

Patrick John Ireland

GW00647525

Cambridge University Press

CAMBRIDGE
LONDON · NEW YORK · MELBOURNE

About the author
Patrick John Ireland MSIAD is a fashion designer
and illustrator. He lectures at the London College
of Fashion and is a visiting lecturer to many places
in Britain and abroad.

The author would like to thank Miss Patricia
Wedderburn for her help with the technical terms
of fashion.

Cover illustrations
The back cover is a design development sheet,
illustrating the development of the two designs
shown on the front cover.

Published by the Syndics of the Cambridge University Press
The Pitt Building, Trumpington Street, Cambridge CB2 1RP
Bentley House, 200 Euston Road, London NW1 2DB
32 East 57th Street, New York, NY 10022, USA
296 Beaconsfield Parade, Middle Park, Melbourne 3206, Australia

© Cambridge University Press 1979

First published 1979

Printed in Malta by
Interprint Limited

ISBN 0 521 21993 0

Contents

Introduction

This book introduces some of the basic principles of fashion design. It is intended to help the student to develop the skills of creating and communicating design ideas. The designer must, of course, have a general awareness of fashion and a sound knowledge of fabrics and the use of colour. He should be able to find inspiration from many sources and then develop these ideas if he is to create original and successful designs. He must have a knowledge of pattern cutting and methods of making up.

Many students of design find it difficult at first to express their ideas on paper and need to acquire some fashion drawing technique. It is hoped that this book and its companion *Fashion Drawing* will be helpful as an introduction. Costume and life classes should also be attended. However, this is not always easy to arrange, a fact taken account of in these pages.

The book is arranged in sections covering different stages in the design process and illustrating basic design features. It shows how design ideas can be developed and includes examples of design briefs and suggestions for projects and further study. The figure guides on the inside of the front and back covers can be used for tracing and copying but should, of course, be dispensed with as skill and confidence increase.

The design process

The design brief

It is important to consider your brief carefully before attempting to produce any design ideas. You must think about all of the following.

Occasion
What sort of occasion are you designing for? Will it be formal or informal, smart or casual? Will the garment be worn for a particular activity, such as sport or dancing?

Season
Are you designing for warm weather or cold, indoor or outdoor wear?

Fabric
This may be part of your brief or you may be able to choose for yourself. Colour, pattern, drape, texture and weight are all very important in a design. The designer must consider the fabric from the point of view of the actual making of the garment. Another important practical aspect is the sort of care the garment will need. Will it need ironing, dry-cleaning or hand-washing, for example? Should it be hardwearing? Are you designing for coolness or warmth?

Image
Who are you designing for? What age range? Should you be aiming for a smart look or a casual look, and so on?

Style features, design details, decorations and trimmings
Sometimes your brief will include suggestions. Sometimes you will need to think these out for yourself. They must be part of your whole design. Do not add them as afterthoughts.

Inspiration and ideas
These come from many different sources. Always be on the look-out for new ideas. Keep a sketch book. Collect cuttings from newspapers and magazines. Collect fabric samples and experiment with them. Detailed suggestions are given throughout the book and in the 'Further study' section at the end.

Selecting fabrics

Make a selection considering weight, drape, texture, colour and pattern. Prepare a *fabric board* arranging samples in groups. Contrast and combine colours, tones and textures. Add trimmings such as ribbons, cords, braids and lace. Experiment with different combinations and decide which you might use in your design.

Sources of inspiration

When working on a new collection a designer needs a source of inspiration for developing his ideas. He will use many areas of research such as paintings, flowers, architecture, films, ballet, opera, and travel to different parts of the world.

As a student of design it is important to be aware of the influences that are affecting fashion: new leisure and sporting activities, entertainments, technology and science, for example. All these things have an influence on the way we live and the clothes we wear.

Make sketches in your sketch-book of anything that interests you or you feel may be useful. These little sketches — plant-forms, decoration, anything that catches your eye or imagination — may later be a source of inspiration for a new design theme.

Design development

Start by working on a silhouette as a theme. Adapt it in different ways. Sketch details: think of the different ways they can be introduced. Think of the back and side views. Consider the most effective ways of using your fabric. Study the way in which it falls and gathers. When you have taken one idea as far as you can, start on a new theme using the same basic ideas and fabric collection. It is this part of the process that the following pages cover.

Creating silhouettes

The silhouette or shape of a garment is created by the skill of the cut and the use of fabrics. The texture of the fabric chosen has a strong influence.

Compare the soft drape of jersey, silk and chiffon to the firmer lines of tweed, linen and taffeta.

Many shapes are created by the use of padding, linings and trimmings. Five silhouettes are illustrated.

Lines within the silhouette

Seams help to create the shape of the garment and produce lines within the silhouette. Lines may be used to achieve decorative effects. The seam may be picked out in many ways, for example piping, braids or top stitching. Some different effects are illustrated here. Note the use of the lines and the different effects of diagonals, verticals and horizontals. Choose other silhouettes and explore the effect of lines on them.

Proportion and balance

The proportion and balance of a design is the relationship of each part to the whole silhouette. Note the proportion of the shapes in the designs illustrated and the balance of colour and pattern used. Many adaptations of one design may be achieved with different colour and pattern combinations.

Methods of fitting

Darts fit and shape a garment. They may be placed at any angle. Sometimes a number of small darts take the place of one large dart. All darts on the bodice are centred to the bust point. Darts usually end in waist, shoulder, centre-front and side seams.

Gathers are used to control the fullness of the material in bodice, skirt and sleeves.

Tucks are folds of fabric arranged in groups providing shape and used as a decorative feature.

Pleats of different styles control the fullness of the fabric.

Seams can incorporate darts and control the shape.

Yokes on a bodice or skirt, control fullness and give a neat fitting.

yokes

seams

gathers

centre-front darts

side darts from side seam

shoulder and waist darts

tucks

pleats

6

Design details

The design details are features of a design that add interest, as illustrated above. It is important to consider the balance of the whole design. The details must be a part of it, not afterthoughts.

Focal points

The focal point on a design is the feature that one would notice first. This can be a design detail at the neck, waist or hem of a garment, or the way in which the fabric and pattern are used.

Surface decoration

Surface decoration is an important consideration. It has many uses. With experience, a designer progresses from using surface decoration as a border at neck, sleeves or hem to discover more exciting and imaginative ways of introducing decoration as an essential part of a design.

The choice of trimmings is wide, and when selecting them the designer must consider with care the fabric to which they will be applied. Trimmings may be used to emphasise the shape of a pocket, yoke or collar; they may add interest to the hem of a skirt or sleeve. Appliqué work and hand or machine embroidery are skilled crafts by means of which many attractive effects can be achieved.

The designer may create many pleasing effects using smocking, shirring, pleating, quilting, pintucks or gathers. These techniques alter the fabric surface, creating new and exciting surface effects (see pp. 30–1).

Focal points

The design development sheet

After carefully considering the design brief you have been given and making your fabric selection, the next stage is to work out your ideas on a design development sheet. Make many sketches as you explore the possibilities of your chosen theme. Think about and draw details such as fastenings and surface decorations at the same time as you work at the overall look of your design and aspects such as line, silhouette and proportion. Make notes and experiment with fabric samples as you go along.

Working in this way you will be able to decide which ideas to drop and which to develop further. You will use the best of these in your production and presentation drawings.

The production drawing

When you have developed the design you want, the next stage is to do a complete analytical working drawing. This gives full information on fabric, cut, style, features and trimmings. It is used by the pattern cutter and the production team who make up the sample garment. This final stage in the design process is not dealt with here. But the book covers the development and communication of design ideas up to the point where they can be finally put on paper for the production process to begin.

The presentation drawing

This drawing is done after the production drawing is completed. It is the one shown to clients and buyers, and used for advertising purposes. It illustrates the complete design and its fashion image.

Design brief

Design a collection of three summer dresses in striped fabrics using the stripes in a variety of ways as in the drawings. Use a plain fabric for contrast.

Striped fabrics come in many different designs and colour combinations. They can suggest many design ideas and can be used to create flattering illusions. Pleats, tucks and cutting on the cross produce a great range of effects.

Lines may be used to flatter the figure. Vertical lines draw the eye up and give an impression of tallness. Horizontal lines have a broadening effect. Always study the fabric carefully and visualise the direction the stripes will take in your design. Consider their effect.

Before you begin consider the possibilities carefully. Remember to put into effect the ideas and techniques suggested on the preceding pages.

It would be helpful to collect a selection of striped and plain fabric samples from which to develop your own design. Make a fabric board relating the plain and striped fabrics to each other.

Decide on the most effective ways of using the fabrics.

Either sketch your designs freely or use tracings of a simple basic figure like those at the front and back of the book. Sketch your designs over the basic figure working in the style illustrated above.

A selection of necklines and armhole shapes cut into the bodice of a garment

Armhole shape

Many effects can be achieved. The armholes can be designed to take a sleeve or to be sleeveless and offer all sorts of design possibilities. Look at the shapes illustrated. Create some more for evening dresses.

Design brief

Design three sleeveless summer dresses concentrating on neck and armhole shapes. Make your own choice of fabric, colour and pattern. Decide whether you are designing for formal or informal occasions. Will the garment be worn on the beach, in the office or, maybe, at parties?

set-in

raglan

kimono

Sleeves

There are many possible variations but they are all based on the three main styles: set-in, raglan and kimono. A wide selection of sleeves is illustrated here and throughout the book. Note how the designs range from very full to tight-fitting. Note how interest can be added at cuff or sleeve head. Tucks, pleating, gathers and draping may all be used to good effect.

Sleeve styles

Kimono sleeve: cut in one with the body of the garment as in a Japanese kimono.

Set-in sleeve: cut separately from the bodice of the garment and fitted into the armhole shape.

Raglan sleeve: extends to the neckline and has slanting seamlines from underarm to neck in front and back.

Sketch book

Make a collection of sleeve styles. Sketch them when visiting museums, looking in shops, reading magazines. These sketches will be invaluable when you come to develop your own designs.

12

*A selection of dresses with sleeve interest as a feature
of the design*

13

stand and fall collar
with separate neckband

Eton collar
with stand

shirt collar
with stand

stand
collar

stand collar

mandarin collar

stand collar
with lapels

stand
collar

break
line

collar

stand

fall

style
line

lapel

Collars

The collar is an important fashion feature. It may
be a functional and very essential part of a garment
designed for warmth and protection from the
weather or it may serve purely as a decorative
feature. It is often made in a contrasting fabric
such as fur or leather. The possibilities for shape
and surface decoration are endless.

There are many different collars derived from a
few basic styles. These may vary considerably from
standing high round the neck to lying flat on the
shoulders. Effects may range from soft to very
sharp and tailored. The collar may be designed with
or without a lapel. Often collars are designed to be
worn with scarves or ties. They may convert to be
worn open or closed or to combine with a decorative
feature at the neck.

Observe the many different styles and how they
are designed for a particular garment. The collar can
be a focal point. The designer should also consider
the practical aspects of the collar, bearing in mind
the activity or environment for which he is designing.

The following terms are used in describing collars.

The *stand* is that part of a collar which fits to the
back of the neck and is covered by the *fall* of the
collar. The stand gives the collar its height.

The *style line* is the shape of the outer edge of the
collar.

The *fall* is that part of the collar which falls over the
stand.

The *break line* is the line on which the lapels turn
back and the *fall* turns over the *stand*.

Some variations of the flat collar

Basic collar styles

Stand collars stand upright from the neckline without a fall. Mandarin collars are stand collars.

Stand and fall collar: also known as a 'collar with stand'. This collar turns down sharply at the break line. A shirt collar is a good example.

Flat collars are cut to lie flat on the shoulders. They have no stand and very little roll.

Shirt collar: turns down from the stand. It is often used on blouses and dresses as well as shirts.

Eton collar: a large turned-over collar of stiffened white fabric. The smaller boys at Eton College still wear the original Eton collar.

Mandarin collar: a small standing collar as seen originally on the gowns worn by Chinese mandarins.

Peter Pan collar: a flat round collar made in one or two pieces. It is attached to the neck edge with a bias strip or fitted facing.

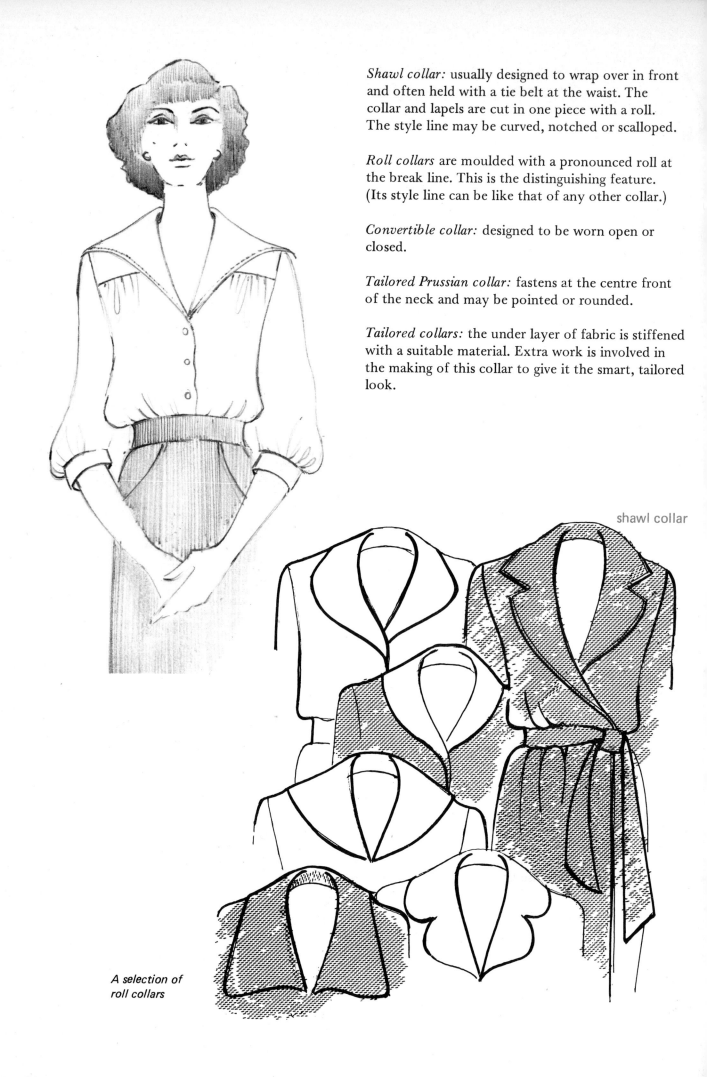

Shawl collar: usually designed to wrap over in front and often held with a tie belt at the waist. The collar and lapels are cut in one piece with a roll. The style line may be curved, notched or scalloped.

Roll collars are moulded with a pronounced roll at the break line. This is the distinguishing feature. (Its style line can be like that of any other collar.)

Convertible collar: designed to be worn open or closed.

Tailored Prussian collar: fastens at the centre front of the neck and may be pointed or rounded.

Tailored collars: the under layer of fabric is stiffened with a suitable material. Extra work is involved in the making of this collar to give it the smart, tailored look.

shawl collar

A selection of roll collars

stand — rolling line

lapel

convertible collar

tailored collars

tailored Prussian collar

17

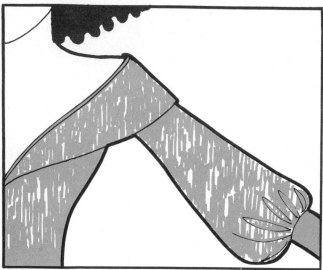

Full set-in sleeve gathered into a deep cuff

Halter neckline

Three-quarter raglan sleeves, gathered into a cuff

Set-in full circular sleeves

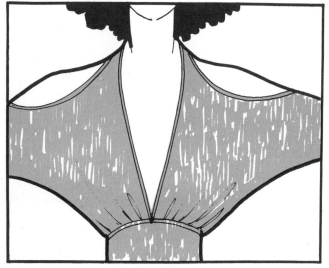

Kimono sleeve with cut out sections on the shoulder

Off-the-shoulder neckline with a gathered frill

Sleeves and necklines

The neckline on a garment is a very important feature and often the focal point in a design. The designer can create many effects with different shapes and trimmings. Illustrated above are some designs showing the way a sleeve or armhole shape may compliment the neckline. Note the use of piping, flounces and frills.

Design brief

Design a collection of up to six tops and skirts suitable for a holiday in a very hot climate.

Things to consider

Occasion: beach and evening wear
Season: summer

Fabrics
Colour
Texture
Pattern
} own choice

Style features: gathers and flounces
Trimming: rouleau
Fashion image: young, feminine

Pockets

Apart from their obvious usefulness, pockets can also be an attractive style feature or focal point in a design. Many effects can be achieved. Size, shape and placing are all important considerations.

When working on a garment a designer must always consider the occasion for which it is to be worn. In some garments, for example sports or work clothing, the pockets may have some special use. Then observations and notes should be made on the activity and the environment in which the garment is to be worn before the design is started.

Patch pocket: sewn onto the material. Many variations of shape are possible. Design details can be added too. The drawings show different-shaped pockets with seams, pin tucks, pleats and piping.

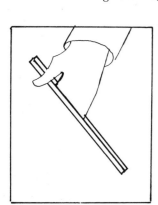

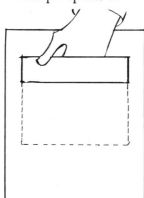

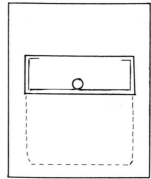

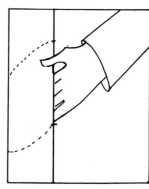

Slit pocket: a slit pocket with buttonhole finish; can be placed at different angles.

One-piece welt: a pocket opening with an upstanding strip or welt.

Slit with flap: a slit pocket with a flap which may have a variety of shapes and decorations.

Seam pocket: concealed in the seams of the garment; particularly effective when a clean line is wanted.

Design brief

Design a collection of up to six casual trouser out-
fits in two colours introducing pockets as a design
feature.

Things to consider
Season: autumn
Fabric: linen
Colour: current fashion colours
Texture: own choice
Style features: pockets
Fashion image: casual, sporty

Pleats

Pleats are folds of fabric, usually made lengthwise. They are used for design effects or for fitting. They may be used in many ways on the skirt, sleeve or bodice. They may vary in their width, depth and arrangement. The pattern, weave and weight of the fabric will also create different effects.

Accordion pleats: are straight and narrow. They resemble the creased folds in the bellows of an accordion.

Box pleats are a combination of two flat folds in opposite directions with the turned under edges meeting underneath. Arranged in a series, the box pleats form inverted pleats on the underside.

Inverted pleats are the reverse of box pleats. The edges meet on the outside of the garment. This pleat may be in a seam, set into the garment or applied. Unlike box pleats, inverted pleats are not used in series.

Knife pleats are narrow folds turned to one side.

Simulated pleats are lines pressed or stitched to imitate the line of a pleat.

Sunray pleats are accordion pleats that are narrow at the top and wider at the bottom. The fabric is pleated on the bias. The pleats radiate from a centre producing a flare.

Unpressed pleats are soft pleats with edges rounded and left unpressed.

Design brief

Design a collection of four blouses and long skirts to go with them. Introduce pleating as a feature.

Occasion: evening wear
Season: spring
Fabric ⎫
Texture ⎬ own choice
Colours ⎭

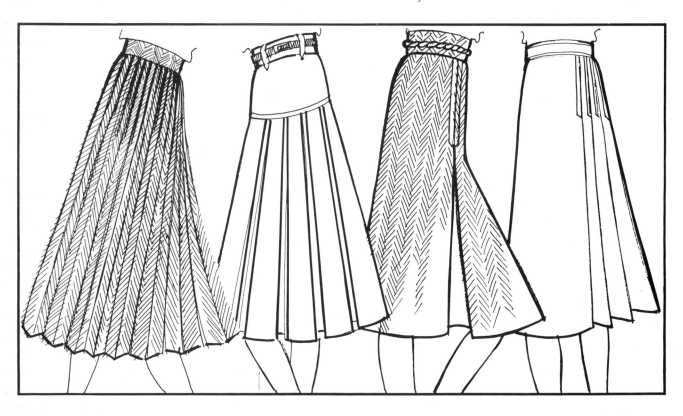

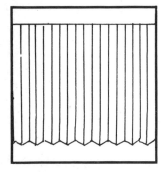

Accordion pleats

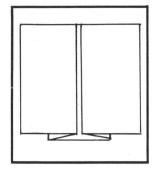

Inverted pleat

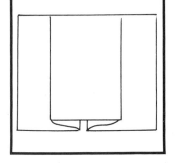

Box pleat

Knife pleats

A selection of blouses using pleats as a feature of the design

Sunray pleats

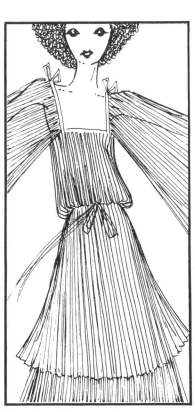

Simulated pleats

Unpressed pleats

Yokes

The yoke can be used in many ways in the design of a dress, skirt, coat or jacket. It may be introduced at shoulders, bodice, waist or hips. It may control fullness or conceal the darts between the yoke and the body of the garment. The shape will vary according to the design. For instance, a yoke can be designed with gathers or without. Emphasis may be given by adding surface interest within the shape of the yoke. Many effects may be achieved

with smocking, shirring, pin tucks, pleating and quilting or the use of contrasting colours, patterns and textures. The outline of the yoke may also be trimmed with piping, braids or lace, etc.

In the above designs the yoke is combined with kimono sleeves; the gathers and piping emphasise the shape.

In the design development sheet opposite the yoke has been adapted to vary the design at waist, bodice and shoulder.

24

Design development sheet

Note how this dress has been developed from a basic idea by adapting the yoke shapes and variations of sleeves, yokes with gathers and peplums.

The peplum is a separate flared piece of fabric extending from the waist to the hip line.

Shoulder yokes with smocking

Scallops edged with piping

Piping and gathers

Shoulder yokes with smocking

Smocking edged with piping

Piping and gathers

Design brief

Design three evening tops with separate skirts featuring yoke interest with gathers.

Occasion: a dinner party and dancing
Fabric: plain jersey, crêpe or silk
Colours: own choice (contrasting colours or tones of one colour)

Remember when designing to consider the draping qualities of the fabric you are designing for. Do not forget to consider the back view and details like openings and fastenings.

When creating designs for a particular fabric, it is a good idea to drape the fabric on a dress stand using pins in order to experiment with the different possibilities of fold, drape, gathering and pleating.

Costume study

Study the clothes of different historical periods. Note the materials, colours, patterns and trimmings used. Try to work out how the garments were cut and look carefully at the shapes achieved. Look at paintings and prints in art books and illustrated history books as well as books on the history of costume. Go to museums, art galleries and exhibitions. Look at the costumes in films and plays and see if you think the designers have been successful. This research will help you to develop ideas of your own.

Observe current fashions — look in shop windows, magazines and newspapers. Note the new colours and images that the advertisers and fashion writers are promoting. What do you think of them?

Developing ideas

Develop your ideas around a theme. From one idea many may develop. Keep on exploiting the possibilities of an idea and experimenting with different effects until you have taken the design as far as you feel you can.

How you work on your ideas depends on your sketching ability and your personal taste. Various ways of sketching are illustrated throughout this book. Some of these effects can be achieved by using the figure guides at the beginning and end of the book, some by free-hand sketching. Use pencils, pens, crayons or paints. Develop your own approach to different design problems.

Design drawings produced by working over a figure guide

1856—60

1852—6

1829—31

Fashion details

Appliqué

The technique of applying the design of one fabric to a second fabric.

Bias

The line taken in folding or cutting material diagonally across warp and weft threads. In fabric, a diagonal line running at an angle of 45° to the selvage.

Cowl drape

The fabric is cut on the bias to form soft folds. The effects can vary from a very full draped cowl to a few soft folds.

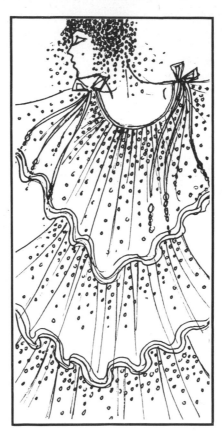

Gathers

Gathers can be attractive on bodice, sleeve or skirt. Many effects are possible, depending on the kind of fabric used and the amount gathered.

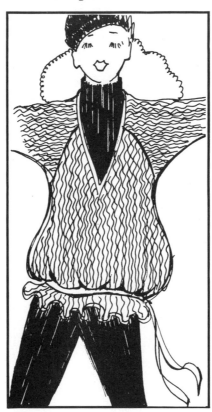

Knitting

Knitting has recently become important in the fashion industry.

The effects of hand and machine knitting are varied by the use of striking patterns, colours and textures. Part of a design may be knitted, or the complete garment.

Patchwork

Patchwork can be made from many different fabrics and patterns. The patches are cut out in selected shapes and stitched together. The pattern of the garment is cut from the patchwork piece as from any length of fabric.

Pin tucks

Pin tucks are folds sewn into the fabric. They are used for decorative effect, to hold fullness and to give shape. Tucks can be of various widths and can be arranged in many ways. They can be used on bodice, skirt or sleeve.

Piping

Cord covered with bias-cut fabric. It can be most effective as a surface decoration or set into a seam.

Quilting

Fine running stitches or machine stitches made through two thicknesses of material with lightweight padding between.

Rouleau

A roll or fold of ribbon or fabric.

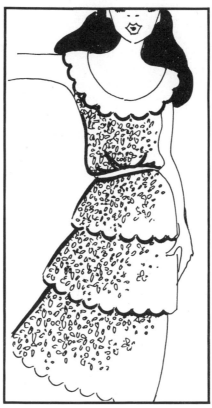

Scallops

Scallops may be edged with a contrasting piping to emphasise the shape. This effect can look attractive on hemlines of skirts and on sleeves and collars.

Shirring

An effect created by sewing elastic thread into the material.

Smocking

A decorative method of gathering together a piece of fabric in regular folds. A number of stitches may be used to achieve decorative effects and they can be combined with many coloured threads. With a patterned fabric the effect can be very pleasing. Pliable fabrics are most suitable for smocking though certain other fabrics such as felt may look effective for some designs.

Further study

Collect fabric samples, press-cuttings, photographs and drawings, pictures of historical costumes.

Observe shop window displays, fashion shows, clothes other people wear, films, television.

Visit art galleries, museums, costume collections, exhibitions.

Discuss fashion industry, mass production, couture, current fashions, fashion influences, fabrics and fashion, sources of inspiration, history of fashion, designers of today, designing for specific purposes (e.g. uniforms, sports wear, industry), images (e.g. designing for the larger fitting, fashion for different ages, fashion for men).

Find out about designers, fashion trends, fabrics, collections, a selected period of history and its influence on fashion today.

Study and read about history of fashion, fashion designers, drawing, the use of colour.

Collect fashion sketches: keep a folder of sketches from magazines, newspapers and pattern books. Study the illustrators' techniques and the many different styles.

Keep a sketch book: make drawings, for reference, of anything which you may find useful in your own designing. It may be a complete garment that catches your eye, or the smallest detail.

Experiment if you are able to sew and use a machine. Take samples of fabric and experiment with them creating different effects with smocking, shirring, pleats, gathers etc. Note how the pattern and texture of the fabric changes with the different processes. This exercise can suggest many new creative ideas for your designs.

Fashion courses

Many courses are available leading to a range of qualifications. Evening classes or one- and two-year courses provide for students aiming to take City and Guilds examinations in dress and allied subjects. Colleges also offer diploma, BA and MA courses lasting up to four years. Most college courses require a number of O-level and, often, A-level passes for entry. Short courses and evening classes are arranged in many areas for people with a general interest in fashion, but who are not looking for professional qualifications. When considering further education in fashion it is advisable to investigate the courses offered carefully. Different courses require different qualifications and also concentrate on different aspects of fashion design, and fashion generally.

A course may include subjects such as life drawing, three-dimensional work, fashion drawing and design, pattern cutting, grading and modelling, textiles, millinery, knitting and embroidery. It may include up to a year spent in industry. Some courses are more closely involved with the fashion industry than others and place greater emphasis on technical and management aspects. Some are concerned with the more creative aspects of the fashion trade.

If you are being interviewed for a course you will be required to produce a portfolio containing examples of your art work. The interviewing panel will not be looking for fashion work especially; they will want to see examples of your general artistic ability. But it is worth including examples of fashion work if you have done some. Select what you show carefully and remember that presentation is very important. Your art teacher will be able to advise you here.

Books for further reading and the library

P.J. Ireland: *Basic Fashion Design* (Batsford)
P.J. Ireland: *Fashion Design Drawing* (Batsford)
P.J. Ireland: *Fashion Drawing in Advertising* (Batsford)
P.J. Ireland: *Drawing and Designing Menswear* (Batsford)
P.J. Ireland: *Drawing and Designing Children's and Teenage Fashions* (Batsford)
W.M. Bull: *Basic Needlework* (Longman)
Basic Tailoring (Time Life)
D. Teague & A. Nicholas: *Embroidery in Fashion* (Pitman)
J. Laver: *Concise History of Costume* (Thames & Hudson)
D. Yarwood: *English Costume* (Batsford)
E. Ewing: *History of Twentieth Century Fashion* (Batsford)
M. Garland: *The Changing Form of Fashion* (Dent)
G. Howell: *In Vogue* (Allen Lane)
H. Stanley: *Modelling and Flat Pattern Cutting* (Hutchinson)
I. Nelms: *Fashion and Clothing Technology* (Hulton Educational Publications)